# Planning for Disaster

*A Business Survival Guide*

## Harry Flowers

ISBN-13: 978-1516911202

ISBN-10: 1516911202

## **<u>Dedication</u>**

I'd like to thank my wife, Karen, for editing the book and being so gracious about the time I spent writing it. Also thanks to John Gill for reviewing it before publishing and Donnie Webb for pointing out the Fujita Scale for rating tornadoes had been replaced with the Enhanced Fujita Scale.

# Contents

# Preface

Disasters happen.  In the last decade, here's a list of just a few:

| Year | Disaster | Location | Fatalities |
|------|----------|----------|-----------|
| 2015 | Earthquake | Nepal | 8,800 |
| 2014 | Flood | Kashmir Valley | 441 |
| 2013 | Typhoon Haiyan (Yolanda) | Philippines | 10,000 |
| 2012 | Hurricane Sandy | Atlantic basin, NY, NJ (US) | 159 |
| 2011 | Tornadoes (523) | Southeast/Midwest US | 498 |
| 2011 | Tsunami | Japan | 19,000 |
| 2010 | Earthquake | Haiti | 314,000 |
| 2008 | Earthquake | China's Sichuan province | 87,000 |
| 2008 | Cyclone Nargis | Myanmar | 138,000 |
| 2005 | Earthquake | Pakistan and Kashmir | 80,000 |
| 2005 | Hurricane Katrina | New Orleans, Louisiana (US) | 1,833 |

While the loss-of-life consequences are immeasurable, the economic and business impact of these disasters is also enormous. The economic impact doesn't always correspond to the extent of the devastation.  Looking at hurricanes, the economic impact of Hurricane Katrina was estimated to be $125 billion and Hurricane Sandy was $65 billion, while Cyclone Nargis' estimated economic impact was $10 billion and Typhoon Haiyan's was around $6 billion.  The death tolls are often higher in areas with poor construction.  The economic impact is usually higher in more developed areas. Whether you're talking deaths or impact on the living conditions and livelihood of those left alive, it's not a situation you want to be in.  But, since disasters happen, it's best to be as prepared for them as you can.  As Benjamin Franklin said, **"By failing to prepare, you are preparing to fail."**

How many businesses fail to recover after a disaster or data loss? In my searches, I've seen quotes of anywhere from 40% to 94% failure rate in the two years following the loss, but I was unable to verify the research or the data was more than ten years old. **One thing *is* certain, though – you don't want your business to contribute to this huge failure statistic.**

If you are involved in creating or maintaining a disaster recovery (DR) plan, keep reading! It wasn't until I was tasked with leading a project team to develop a new DR plan that I realized it really required several prerequisites to do properly.

Back in the days of mainframes and minicomputers, it was fairly straightforward for an IT department to create a DR plan that would meet business needs in the event their computing resources were unavailable. You basically needed more systems somewhere else like the ones you had, backup tapes to restore there, and a way for users to connect terminals to them. Then, you could recreate the datacenter and thus recreate your IT environment.

The rise of the personal computer (PC) began to change things. Microcomputer servers began taking more and more of the workload and people weren't just using their PC's to run a terminal emulator to connect to corporate resources. Tasks ran on people's desktop systems and a rapidly growing number of microcomputer servers were doing the heavy lifting. The diversity and complexity of the IT environment grew exponentially.

Why am I rehashing all this? It's because some folks still want to make their DR plans as if nothing has changed in the last decades. It's not just the servers in the datacenter that changed; the entire environment has changed and keeps changing. With increasing "bring your own device" (BYOD) computing including more and more mobile devices of all sorts, the diversity and complexity keeps increasing. Adding cloud computing resources into the mix makes things even more challenging despite what some well-meaning pundits will tell you (more on that in the DR chapter).

The point is this: determining the scope of what your disaster recovery plan needs to cover requires a careful business impact analysis and risk analysis. If you start in the datacenter and work backwards, you are going to miss things that don't take place there but may be just as critical to your recovery. You'll totally miss non-IT services, too.

If you want to have a plan that will really help your business when things go wrong, that takes work and preparation. This book is intended to help guide you through the process of creating plans and procedures that could save your business.

 Warning!
Geek
Speak

In the course of this book, I'll put this warning before the more technical information. People who aren't interested in the more technical content can safely skip these sections or save them for late-night reading when you are having trouble getting to sleep. When the snooze section is over, you'll see this:

 Returning You
to Non-Geek
Speak ☺

# Chapter 1:
# Executive Support

**The first step in contingency planning is getting the chief officers to form a consensus on making it a priority.** This step is crucial to creating a successful plan. Without their support, the time required for their staff to work on the remaining steps won't be forthcoming. An outline of the process you will use should be presented and approved by your executive board before you start.

Prince Charles of England said, "There's nothing like a jolly good disaster to get people to start doing something." This seems to be borne out by having the biggest pushes for disaster planning seem to be *after* a disaster. **Be among the prudent who plan ahead.**

Even if you're the chief information officer (CIO), you will need the support of your peers to create good contingency plans. If it is not a shared priority to create realistic contingency plans, you will likely fail to complete a business impact analysis (BIA) with a policy in place to update it for each new service or application. Without that, too many of your organization's business needs will very likely be overlooked in the planning process.

It's easy to just skim over this part of the book and say, "Yeah, we've got the executives behind this." You can read of my misadventures in executive support in the chapter on disaster recovery planning. This is just a friendly caution that it may bite you later if you find you don't have enough support to interrupt your key business managers for their valuable input into the process. The best way they'll make it a priority is if their bosses believe it's a priority.

## Contingency Planning Isn't Just about IT

There are many parts of contingency planning that aren't about technology at all. When we get to the risk assessment portion, some of the disasters you might be planning for have human consequences far beyond use of technology. The basics of food, shelter, and clothing after devastating disasters such as hurricanes and earthquakes come first. Once the human necessities are met, the basic business needs can be addressed. Other disasters such as tornadoes and fires may just affect a localized area where your business site (or one of them) is located. Office relocation, transportation, and housing (if workers must be relocated away from their homes) are all non-IT business needs that also must be considered in the event of a disaster. It's best if all the business units in your organization work together on contingency planning.

## Contingency Planning Isn't Just an IT Project

In addition to the non-IT portions of contingency planning, doing the IT planning with no input from the people who use your information technology (IT) services will severely cripple your plans. Unless your business has only a few employees, then you can't know what and how everyone uses technology in the performance of their jobs. The most time-intensive part of this for the non-IT groups will be the business impact analysis (BIA).

As I mentioned in the preface, a lot of the technology within your organization may be outside your datacenter. For some outsourced services, your centralized IT folks might not have been involved at all. It's also a safe bet that even for services IT provides, you may not realize everything that depends on those services.

There may be some reluctance to discuss non-IT-department supported services, especially if a few rules were bent or procedures ignored to provide them. Sometimes this is referred to as "shadow IT". This might also occur for unofficial projects started within IT. Several years ago, this was often true of projects using open source software. What starts out as an investigation or trial starts being used and before you know it, you're depending on it for a service. Work out the politics surrounding the services and encourage departments to include everything. Perhaps granting amnesty for any non-sanctioned service or grandfathering any existing services would help open the discussions. **It's time to bring shadow IT into the light and examine it.** You might even decide to officially support such projects in the future. I know some folks would consider not having disaster planning a just penalty for implementing shadow IT projects, but that's not really in your organization's best interests.

From a project management standpoint, I recommend creating a contingency planning project with several sub-projects, one for each of the plans that comprise it. Until the contingency plan is "finished" (by "finished", I mean each sub-project goes through completion with no changes at least once), each of the sub-projects may influence changes in any of the others. Each plan should be reviewed until you can cycle through all of them without making any changes. Then, the overall project is complete and you place your policy and procedures for keeping it updated in action. **Contingency planning has to be an ongoing process because it can quickly become outdated as your use of technology changes.**

If you draw a network diagram of your project plan dependencies, you'll notice that some of them can be going on at the same time. Your Risk Analysis isn't dependent upon your Business Impact Analysis and vice versa, so those sub-projects can proceed at the same time. Much of the work on Business Continuity and Disaster Recovery plan sub-projects can also take place in parallel, though they can have some impact on each other. From the beginning, you can work on policies and procedures to ensure that changes to services and new services are updated in your plans – you want them available for approval before the full project end.

## No Magic Wand or Crystal Ball

"Anything worth doing is worth doing well."[1] If you invest the time and effort needed for thorough planning into making your contingency plans, you'll reap the benefits. There aren't any shortcuts worth taking in this process. Here are the two possible outcomes:

1. No disasters strike and you don't need the plans. You come away with a better understanding of your business and remove unnecessary risks from your environment. You also pass the contingency planning parts of audits with flying colors.
2. Disaster strikes and you're prepared. You probably save your company from going out of business, your jobs (even if your company stays in business, being caught unprepared would likely cause some firings), and possibly even lives.

Thus, contingency planning is a win-win proposition. Give it the time and effort it deserves.

There is a recent trend to down-play the need for thorough disaster planning, either by shortcuts or generalized plans that are not specific enough to be tested. These folks are willing to accept the risk of disasters without adequate plans. Even if disaster should strike, if they change jobs every few years, they figure they'll be gone from one where they had responsibility or they will be too new in the current one to have to accept responsibility (their predecessor is to blame). This is both a selfish and short-sighted approach.

None of us has a crystal ball to gaze into the future. However, we do know this:

1. Disasters will happen.
2. No one has immunity from disaster.

Wishful thinking that they'll always happen elsewhere isn't any more realistic than holding to Murphy's Law[2] that they'll always happen.

## Think Strategically

One thing to do after all phases of your contingency planning are completed is look at your plan from a strategic viewpoint. It can point out vulnerabilities in your business planning. For example, if your business deals with the manufacture or sale of luxury goods for one region, you might see that you would lose your customer base for an extended period of time with some of the disaster scenarios. You might consider diversifying into some essential product areas or expanding your market into more geographic locations, if feasible.

If you are a global business, the resiliency expectations on your company are going to be much higher than a local business after a disaster. Basically, the farther your customers are removed from the area of the disaster, the less impact they'll find acceptable. Even if you have datacenters distributed around the world, if the design assumes your headquarters datacenter is functional, you've got a potential problem.

As part of the contingency planning project wrap-up, you might find it advantageous to have the executive committee conduct an interview of the folks on the team with strategic planning in mind. By the end of the process, they're going to have a lot of insight into the strengths and weaknesses across your business. The answers to some insightful questions might reveal opportunities for improvement or expansion or confirm a different direction you'd already been considering. It's also a good place to float such ideas to see the team's reaction to their implementation and what contingency plans might change because of them.

# Chapter 2:
# <u>Business Impact Analysis</u>

The business impact analysis (BIA) is where you identify each service your organization uses and look at the impact on your business if you had to do without it. Ways to mitigate the impact in the short term will become your business continuity plan (BCP), while the steps you will take to fully recover the service will form your disaster recovery (DR) plan. As you can see, it's a critical part of your contingency planning process.

The BIA is the most time-intensive part of contingency planning and requires the most coordination with your entire business. While the first run at this will take the most effort, you also need to redesign your processes so that updating the BIA, if needed, is a part of your change management process. The entire BIA, regardless of application changes, should be reviewed periodically. The period is dependent on how dynamic your environment is. Three-year full reviews are probably fine for many businesses.

## Data for Each Service

For each service, you will collect the following data:

1. A **service name and description** (so everyone is talking about the same thing when discussing it). If you have implemented the Information Technology Infrastructure Library (ITIL) framework, you already have an IT service catalog (or catalogue, since ITIL is of British origin) to use as a great starting point for filling in a few of the items for data collection. Don't depend on it to be an exhaustive list, however, as IT services provided by outside sources might not be catalogued.

2. The primary user of the service as well as who is responsible for providing it. Names and positions for these contacts are important since people come and go more often than you might update the analysis.

3. An indication of how critical it is to the business, such as **critical, severe, moderate,** and **minimal impacts** – this is your **BIA Tier**. Critical impact services are the ones where you can't do any business without them – you might as well close your doors. Severe impact service loss would cripple your business and have large financial impact as well. Moderate impact service losses would likely inconvenience your customers and staff with significant financial impact, while minimal impact losses would be inconvenient to staff and have small financial impact. These are often assigned numerical tiers, so that critical is BIA Tier 1, severe is BIA Tier 2, etc. Four tiers are usually sufficient, but if you find you only need three or it'll take five to really accurately depict your situation, it's best to fit the model to the data and not get too hung up on how many tiers you have. On the other hand, if you decide twenty tiers fits best, you've likely created a level of precision and accuracy that doesn't exist in reality and is also unwieldy to use.

4. The maximum time you can be without the service – this is called the **recovery time objective (RTO)**. It's possible that your business continuity plan (BCP) options will work well enough to extend your RTO for service restoration, so you might re-visit this after your BCP is completed. There may be legal, financial, or regulatory compliance issues involved as well. You may have internal or external service level agreements (SLA) that include support for an implied RTO in the service availability language. If you see "five nines" or percentages for availability, I cover what those mean in Appendix 1.

5. The maximum time of data loss due to the disaster – this is called the **recovery point objective (RPO)**. For

example, daily backups have a RPO capability of about 24 hours.

Warning! Geek Speak

If you have an eight-hour backup window and your last backup started at the beginning of it and the disaster occurred just before the next backup at the end of it, the maximum time of data loss would actually be just under 32 hours for a daily backup.

As another example, if you have remote site replication with data snapshots being taken, your RPO may be as low as the replication time or as high as your snapshot interval, depending on the type of disaster. If the disaster is an important file deleted in error, replication will insure that it was also deleted at the remote site, so you'd be depending on your snapshot to recover it.

Returning You to Non-Geek Speak ☺

If a service has no data component (as is the case with non-IT services) this metric may be omitted.

6. The minimum percentage capacity needed – this is your **recovery capacity objective (RCO)**. If you can get by okay with half the capacity until service is fully restored, you'd have a RCO of 50%. This becomes important when budgeting for disaster recovery options. Note that it's also possible to have a value over 100%; this is typically the case when this service will be used more heavily during recovery such as a chat server for coordinating recovery efforts. I've not seen any literature on disaster recovery that included this item, but it's an important consideration.

7. The **list of other services needed to provide this service**, if any. Business users may know some of them, but the list will need to be completed by IT support. Collaboration between your line-of-business managers and your IT support staff is essential. After all, you can't expect your business users to know what kind of dependence on authentication services their applications have.

Warning!
Geek
Speak

For example, if you have implemented centralized identity management systems and use the central authentication service (CAS) or Shibboleth with it for single sign-on (SSO), those are service dependencies that will need to be taken into account. Likewise the hardware service dependencies (does the application server use local storage or depend on a storage area network (SAN) service)?

Returning You
to Non-Geek
Speak ☺

8. The **list of applications, software, and hardware needed** to provide just this particular service. If it's not an IT service, you'll have a different set of requirements. Don't include hardware or software that makes up another service that you've already listed in the prior item. For IT services, this section is typically completed by your IT department. You may find that, if several services require the same equipment (like the SAN example in the previous item), it's worthwhile to separate that into its own service to avoid multiple duplicate listings. For outsourced services or ones implemented at a cloud vendor site, you

may have limited information beyond the vendor name and location(s).

Ideally, everyone would like an RTO and RPO near zero and RCO of 100%. If money and application design weren't issues, that'd be great! It's not unusual to revisit the BIA once you get to disaster recovery planning and put real money estimates to providing the given RTO, RPO, and RCO for each service. Generally, only your top two tiers rate what often amounts to tripling the hardware and software budgets. It's really best to encourage realistic values for these up front. The BIA is a "living document"; you'll frequently be making changes and additions to it. When presenting it to your users for the data collection phase, make sure they realize that the values they give are subject to further discussion.

While criticality (BIA tier) and low recovery time objectives may seem to go hand-in-hand, there are business factors to consider. For example, in manufacturing, how much inventory is available in warehouses elsewhere may give a "grace period" to get your production lines going again? On the other hand, I have seen both RTO and RPO tied to the BIA tier instead of determined by service. If that works for your business, then that might simplify your business impact analysis process.

A "sanity check" for your BIA is making sure that you **don't have a service on one tier that depends on another one at a lower tier**. If it's a Tier 2 service, then everything it needs has to be either Tier 1 or Tier 2 also. The only exception to this is if there's an easy way to mitigate the need for the lower tier service during its recovery time. Otherwise, the service is really more critical than it'd been designated since more critical services depend on it.

A second "sanity check" is making sure that your **recovery time objectives (RTO) for dependent services are not shorter than the services that they depend upon**. One or the other needs to be adjusted unless your business continuity plan for the depended upon service is good enough to meet the needs of the dependent service during the time gap.

If you're having trouble getting started, there are also many businesses that offer contingency planning services that come with consulting and tools to see the process through. They can help get your BIA done and proceed to the other planning phases. Last time I priced them, the companies I found were not inexpensive, however. Here is a list of some of the advantages to using consultants:

1. Experience and expertise in contingency planning
2. Often have software to aid the process; at least have templates they'll adapt to your organization
3. Unbiased third party for RTO, RPO, and RCO discussions
4. If your corporate culture is one that doesn't respect in-house expertise, you get the credibility of the consulting firm. In my opinion, it's a bad reason, but it is reality in some businesses. Getting the plans completed well is more important than who gets the credit.
5. They can provide recovery services or recommend vendors who do – more about that in the DR chapter. You lose some of that unbiased advantage because they would have financial incentive to over-emphasize more expensive options, so this requires careful handling.

## Data Collection and Organization
The method of data collection should fit in with what your users are comfortable with. Whether you use web forms with a database to hold the information, distribute Word document forms and store them in something like a SharePoint site, or integrate it into some fancy ITIL or IT service management (ITSM) product, you want something that is easily entered and modified. Remember, a BIA by its purpose is a dynamic document, so you want something that users and IT staff can both easily maneuver. You should also have the capability of producing reports that can be distributed to all the key personnel in your recovery documents.

It's best to have a business team (with some IT staff on it) assigned to the BIA who will help each business area when filling out the data for the forms. They can consult on scope and answer questions. It's important not to just turn a data collection site over to someone in each area and expect them to meet a certain deadline. You need to plan guidance through the process. It's also good to have a view of many areas so you can detect early on if one area is either underestimating or overestimating the BIA Tier for their services in comparison to the others in your organization.

As I've already alluded to, requiring time from every area of your business to detail every service they use is not a task to be taken lightly. While it may seem obvious that it's in everyone's best interest to make sure the services on which they depend are covered, you may have to call upon executive support to underscore the importance of full participation. **Time is a precious commodity but so is having plans to save your business.**

## Example Business Impact Analysis

I'm going to take an example that all companies will have from human resources (HR) services. I'll use this example for each of the plans I'm covering in this book. Most of the software to support it is probably a part of a purchased enterprise resource planning (ERP) package, though it's common to use outside sources for employee recruitment these days.

One of the first challenges you'll have is deciding how far to break down the various HR services. If you try to have a single service for it, you'll find that the pieces you do in-house versus the outsourced bits don't work very well in a single service description. You may also consider some HR services to be in different BIA tiers; for example, payroll and recruiting. You likely want payroll to continue no matter what, but you may actually want a pause on recruiting as you're recovering from a disaster.

On the other hand, there may be a temptation to break things down too much. In our payroll example, do you include timekeeping for hourly employees as a part of it or separately? How about leave reporting for salaried employees? Where does information about bonuses or service awards fit in? What about W-4 updates? Transmitting information to the IRS and mailing W-2 forms for tax season?

As you work to fill out your BIA form, you'll find your "happy medium", the balance between trying to cover too much in a single service and being too specific that leads to creating more distinct services than you need. This is where your BIA business team's guidance can really help each business unit break things down into manageable service scopes.

For my example, I'm going to focus on payroll. My fictitious company is going to include time and leave entry, the payroll transmissions to the bank(s), and things that affect that during the year such as tracking the bonuses and W-4 changes which affect withholding every pay period. We're going to push off the IRS transmission and W-2 stuff into our year-end processing.

My fictitious company has both hourly and salaried workers, but no one working on commission (though sales are rewarded through a bonus system). All employees are paid the first business day after the fifteenth and the last business day of every month (twice monthly). This means that payrolls don't change dramatically between pay periods and most exceptions are bonuses.

The next page shows my BIA table for the payroll service.

| Business Impact Analysis | |
|---|---|
| Service | Payroll |
| Description | The payroll service consists of time and leave entry, all deductions and bonuses, and bank transmissions for employee pay. |
| Primary Client | All employees |
| Responsible Party | Shelia Gallivant Compensation Director, HR |
| BIA Tier | 2 - Severe Impact |
| Recovery Time Objective | 1 Month |
| Recovery Point Objective | 1 Day |
| Recovery Capacity Objective | 100% |
| Other Services Needed | Base ERP HR System (for time and leave entry and payroll file generation), LAN Access, and Internet Access (for secure payroll transmittal) |
| Specific Hardware and Software | Windows PC for payroll accountant on network MyBank Secure File Transfer software package installed on PC |

One thing that might stand out is the month-long RTO. Why we can allow up to a month will be clear after looking at our business continuity plan. Another thing that might stand out is the short list of specific hardware and software. Remember, we're not including anything that is a part of another service, in this case, our "Base ERP HR System", that may have a long list of hardware and software dependencies.

# Chapter 3:
# <u>Risk Analysis</u>

One of the keys to planning for disasters is knowing the likely extent of damage in various scenarios. Listing the disaster scenarios is the first step, but how many resources you're willing to dedicate to avoidance or recovery should correspond to the likelihood of the disaster occurring. After all, if you live over a thousand miles from the nearest volcano, that's one scenario you can skip. Likewise for hurricanes if you're that far from the nearest coast.

There are other names for this process, such as *risk assessment*. There are also other names for processes that include this, such as *risk management*. If you're looking at HIPAA compliance issues or ISO certifications, they may have specific meanings other than what is obvious from the wording used. In those contexts, you should use their definitions. For this process, I'll be using risk analysis.

Risk analysis is also not limited to disasters. There are the everyday risks such as those from not getting a project completed on time, not meeting compliance requirements, or losing key personnel. Some companies have positions dedicated to risk analysis. For the purposes of this book, we'll be focusing on the disaster risk analysis aspect of the field.

## Identifying Disasters for Risk Analysis

These come in two main varieties: natural and human. Neither type is particularly predictable. Your organization will have to pick which ones are concerns for your business.

**Examples of Natural Disasters**

1.  Fire (Localized or Wildfires)

    Fire is still one of the most likely of disasters. They can be caused by faulty wiring, natural gas leaks, spontaneous combustion of cleaning rags, lightning strikes, or arson. Hopefully, you already have your datacenter protected by an automatic fire suppression system using a clean agent halocarbon gas.[3] Fires that are the result of earthquakes rupturing gas lines are likely the worst case since there is a low likelihood of any firefighting assistance in a major quake with fires scattered all over the city. Wide-spread wildfires can also cause air-quality issues and evacuations, even if your buildings are spared from the fire itself. If you must evacuate, you'll have to decide whether to do a full shutdown before you go or leave everything running and hope for the best.

2.  Flood (Pipes Bursting, Flash Floods, River Flooding, & Storm Surge)

    Flooding is also high on the list of possible disasters. Even if you live in the desert, flash flooding can be a major problem; Phoenix, Arizona, experienced deadly flooding after receiving a downpour of three inches of rain on September 8, 2014, turning interstate highways into lakes. Most buildings are at risk of plumbing issues that can cause flooding, especially in regards to restrooms.

3.  Tornado/High Winds

    Whether it's a tornado or straight-line winds, you can count on a fairly random path of destruction from where roof shingles have been torn off to all that's left of buildings is basements. When planning for recovery from a tornado, assume that buildings nearby are also damaged or destroyed. The Enhanced Fujita Tornado Intensity Scale is used to rank tornados between EF0 and EF5.[4]

4.  Lightning Strikes

    These have long been the bane of anyone running wires. Fiber optic cables have become the material of choice for networking between buildings because they optically isolate the electricity from traveling along a wire – if only we could do the same for power lines!

5. Hurricane/Typhoon/Cyclone
   According to the U.S. National Oceanic and Atmospheric Administration (NOAA), "The **only difference** between a hurricane, a cyclone, and a typhoon is the **location where the storm occurs**. Hurricanes, cyclones, and typhoons are all the same weather phenomenon; we just use different names for these storms in different places. In the Atlantic and Northeast Pacific, the term 'hurricane' is used. The same type of disturbance in the Northwest Pacific is called a 'typhoon' and 'cyclones' occur in the South Pacific and Indian Ocean."[5] This disaster combines high winds and flooding over a large area. The Saffir-Simpson Hurricane Wind Scale is used to rank them, on a scale from 1 to 5.[6] While a category 4 hurricane only has wind speeds similar to a EF3 tornado, the much larger area and longer period of sustained wind means more damage is likely.

6. Earthquake
   If your region has ever experienced an earthquake, you should have a plan. Occasionally, an earthquake will strike somewhere new, but the majority will be in regions near fault lines where they've happened before. In addition to assigning a likelihood of earthquake, you need to find out the likelihood of various magnitudes. One of the first and most well-known scales of measurement is the Richter scale. The Moment Magnitude scale has largely replaced it in scientific study. Since the Richter and Moment Magnitude scales are base-10 logarithmic, an earthquake measuring six on the scales is one-hundred times more intense than one measuring a four. The distance you are from the epicenter of the quake is also a determining factor for damage, as the intensity dissipates the farther you are from the origin. How much the intensity dissipates

depends on the terrain type. Damage can also be compounded by the terrain type ("unconsolidated soil" tends to liquefy during a quake).[7]

7. Mudslide/Landslide/Avalanche/Sinkhole
All of these disasters occur in geographically-prone areas. Although these can be triggered by earthquakes, there are other triggers as well. Heavy rains are obviously the main triggers for mudslides. There is a rising incidence rate for the last of these, sinkholes. Twenty percent of global land mass has porous bedrock such as limestone, dolomite, and gypsum. Increased demands on water tables in such areas followed by heavy rains are a recipe for disaster. Florida contains many prime examples of this, where many lakes are actually ancient sinkholes. The upshot of all of these is your building(s) may be buried or swept away.

8. Tsunami/Tidal Waves
These waves are caused by large displacements of water. They're sometimes called tidal waves because they resemble a rapid high tide, more so than breaking beach waves. While planning for them is similar to major flash flooding, their occurrence is harder to predict and the expected water level may also be difficult to predict.

9. Volcanic Eruption
Explosions and lava flows, while highly destructive, are usually limited to near the volcano. The more far-reaching damage is usually caused by volcanic ash. At worst, it can accumulate and bury areas (think Pompeii). It can cause low visibility and breathable air quality problems at lower levels. A few inches of ash won't melt like snow; it does settle some but you have to clean it up.

10. Extremes of Unusual Heat/Cold (Blizzards & Ice Storms)
These can be both frustrating and deadly. A heat wave can also cause power issues as every air conditioning unit in the area struggles to keep pace, sometimes unsuccessfully. Extreme cold can cause pipes to freeze and shut down chilled water cooling systems – ironic that your datacenter

may be in danger of overheating when it's bitter cold outside. Ice storms can down power lines, trees, and make travel treacherous with ice-covered roads.

11. Biological Plagues/Epidemics/Pandemics

    While your infrastructure may be untouched, the potential for quarantines and human sickness and death is something that needs to have planning. A few years ago, the avian flu was in the news as a likely pandemic waiting to happen. As I write this, Ebola is in the news and the danger of a possible airborne mutation is frightening. Planning for biological disasters is different from most of the others in that you don't typically assume any loss of equipment. These plans need to include ways to keep people apart to avoid the spread of disease (employees and customers alike) as well as account for a significant portion of your workforce to be unavailable. For employees, enabling them to work from home whenever feasible is one option. If you are in a service industry, finding ways of providing your services to customers without in-person contact is the challenge. You might have a random numbered listing of employees and do a couple of scenarios with them; first, assume the odd-numbered ones are out, then do the same but with the even-numbered ones. Working through those scenarios can help with your planning.

12. Solar Flares/Electromagnetic Pulse (EMP)

    I've read recently about businesses building datacenters that will resist electromagnetic pulses. Whether they're trying to avoid EMP by solar flare or artificially created ones, this is a newer trend. A major solar flare is capable of taking out power grids that would take years to rebuild, but planning for something less severe is also worthwhile. You also could be the target of an EMP generator if someone with the resources would like to disrupt your business; that'd be hard to track down.

A side benefit of shielding against electromagnetic pulses entering your datacenter is that the same shielding also keeps data from being leaked via electromagnetic fields or wirelessly transmitted out, improving overall security.

**Examples of Human Disasters**

1.  Power Outages (Short-Term or Extended)

    These are common enough that most folks use an uninterruptable power source (UPS) that uses batteries to deal with very short power outages. Back that up with a generator and now you have a few days or longer if you're able to refuel it. Making sure the network connectivity is also protected is important. Extended outages over a wide area from causes such as an earthquake or hurricane may force you to abandon the site even if it's otherwise sound.

2.  Hacking – Data Theft

    Data theft is difficult to detect. They're not taking your data, they're taking a copy; it's not like it's missing from your systems. Data theft is often not detected until the leaked data is actually used somewhere and can be traced back to your systems. By then, the hackers could have had run of your servers for many months. Or, it could be an inside job. Most internal hacking is done for data theft. It's much better to secure data by limiting what systems the servers holding the data can communicate with. There are also network monitoring systems that can detect unusual network activity from a server that could lead you to investigate.

3.  Hacking – Data Manipulation or Deletion

    In this case, unlike the prior one, data may be deleted or encrypted and held for ransom. Either way, it's going to be more obvious and definitely malicious. Data manipulation can be more subtle, though. Someone might sabotage your decision support systems by changing the data they're relying on. They could also modify financial data you publish about your company to manipulate the stock price. Other hackers may offer updates to your systems for pay, like deleting parking violations or speeding tickets. Did I mention all this is illegal? Unfortunately, that doesn't stop many hackers.

4. Hacking – Service Disruption
   In this scenario, your servers aren't necessarily compromised. An example of this is a distributed denial of service attack. It works by overwhelming your servers or network rather than breaking into systems. Or rather, it's other people's systems that were hacked to participate in a distributed denial of service against your servers. In any case, your own security may be good but you'll still have to deal with attacks.

5. Human Error – Data Loss and/or Service Disruption
   People make mistakes. They delete files by mistake. They enter erroneous dates for data purges. These aren't insider hackers; they're just folks like you and me that can make mistakes. Sometimes those mistakes can be difficult to fix.

6. Cloud Provider/Outsourcer Failure – Short Term
   Cloud provisioning is gaining by leaps and bounds, but the cloud providers have outages, too. All the big name providers have a history of multi-hour outages, some running to multiple days for at least some customers. These are all cases in which the redundancy they have in place failed to preserve services for their customers. If you can't tolerate this level of downtime for the services they're providing to you, you need a contingency plan of your own for those services.

7. Cloud Provider/Outsourcer Failure – Long Term
   Okay, this can be much scarier than the prior item. What happens if your service disappears because your provider closed its doors? How do you get your data back? Can others read your data if the assets are sold at auction? What about the applications that you used to enter and report on that data? This is an area in which advance preparation is your best chance of preservation. Even if a provider can give you thirty-days' notice, can you really

replace their application and save your data in that time frame?

8. Accidents – Road, Rail, Air (Plane), Water (Barge/Ship)

If you're near a major shipping artery, regardless of mode, you run the risk of some hazardous cargo losing containment. Whether it's a rail car derailment or big rig tanker in a traffic accident, chemical spills can force evacuations for quite some distance. A chlorine gas cloud is bad for people and equipment. It doesn't have to be something that major – you might want to have a plan for traffic stoppages of several hours due simply to car accidents in unfortunate areas. Depending on your business, that may or may not have a major impact.

9. Structural Failures – Buildings, Dams, Bridges, etc.

This might be looked on similar to earthquake damage, but without the quake. It's highly dependent on your location and the state of maintenance of structures. Unfortunately, the infrastructure in the U.S. is in bad need of maintenance for bridges and roads. If you're downstream of a dam, you might want to see how it did on its last inspection (and when that was). A lot of buildings aren't up to current building codes because they only have to be inspected when getting permits for additions or major renovations.

10. Terrorism, Riots, and Warfare

Terrorists can strike anywhere, but they tend to have targets in larger cities. Most urban settings can spawn riots given the right stimulus. If you're in a major city, you might want to develop contingency plans for these. Pretty much anything can happen if you have a war with battles fought within your own borders. While you might not have planning scenarios that include warfare, you should know that most insurance policies don't cover it, either. So, maybe one thing you should plan for is how you recover if your insurance won't pay for rebuilding or replacing whatever is lost. Depending on your location, this last one may be a stretch. However, some of you or your parents may have lived through a war in your location and it's not such a leap to think of it happening again.

## Sorting Through Disaster Impacts

Once you've identified the disasters you should plan for, you need to determine what the impact of each might be. For example, you might have a disaster that just destroys your datacenter; that's possible with a fire contained to the datacenter or flooding due to broken pipes above it. You don't have to have an individual plan for every disaster – the two reasons you started there were these:

1. Risk is based on the likelihood of that disaster. While many disasters may have similar impacts, your planning will take into account the combination of risks from different disaster scenarios for a particular impact.
2. For each disaster, you need to think through the possible impacts. For one like fire, you should think through fires in any building and consider the spread through adjacent buildings before it's brought under control. You should always make one scenario that has your datacenter totally out of commission. If you have multiple datacenters in geographically diverse locations, you should plan for scenarios that would cover each one being destroyed but assume others will be intact.

For most disasters, there's a range of damage that could occur. With hurricanes, you might have one set of impacts for a category 1-3 and another for a category 4-5. The same goes for earthquake magnitudes – you probably want to have a probable impact with 5-6 and another for 7-8 (remember, it's a base-ten logarithmic scale, so each one is ten times worse than the one before it).

Some scenarios will cause destruction so total that an option you might consider is closing the business and starting over. For a small local business in an area that's got widespread destruction over a hundred-mile diameter, that may be a very reasonable approach. No matter the size business, there are some disasters that are so severe, you should probably not make contingency plans for them unless you're a government, such as global thermonuclear war. If your business model won't work in the post-disaster era, then don't waste time and resources on developing a contingency plan for that severe an impact. **Plan for things you can survive.**

## How to Assign Probabilities

When looking at risks, you have to determine a reasonable timeframe over which you expect the risk to occur with a particular probability. For example, the probability of a short-duration power outage tomorrow is much less than an outage sometime over the next ten years. One is unlikely while the other is a near certainty. To establish a reasonable timeframe for contingency planning purposes, you have to look at the longevity of the services you're protecting. If you're looking at datacenter hardware-based services, perhaps a ten-year period is reasonable.

For many of the "major disasters", there are research groups that study them and sometimes publish what they believe the probability of occurrence is. For example, in the mid-south area where the New Madrid seismic zone exists, the Center for Earthquake Research and Information (CERI) at the University of Memphis is a good source of information for disaster planning regarding earthquakes.

While mathematical probabilities can be easily determined by dividing the number of possible outcomes you're interested in by the total number of possible outcomes, disaster risks aren't as deterministic as throwing dice or picking a card out of a deck. Unless you have access to insurance company numerical risk data on disaster risks, you are more likely to be served by general categories:

| Risk Category | Meaning |
|---|---|
| High | This most likely will occur over the specified time period. (greater than a 50% chance) |
| Moderate | This is more likely not to occur than occur, but not by much. You may have already had an occurrence in the past. |
| Low | This is unlikely, but you've seen examples of it occurring in other places similar to your own within the time period you're analyzing. |
| Very Low | This is very unlikely within the specified time period, but it's occurred in the past in places similar to your own. |
| Extremely Low | There have been no occurrences of this in places similar to your own in ten times the time period you're analyzing. |

In addition to past occurrences, there are other conditions that can increase or decrease a risk factor. If the area is in a multi-year drought, the risk of wildfires increases substantially. Some cyclic patterns (such as the 11-year cycle for sunspot activity) are predictable, while others are only noticeable as trends (hurricane activity). If there are conditions that warrant an increase in risk, those need to be taken into account as well as historical data.

Any risks that you categorize as Extremely Low, you can safely omit from the impact portion of your risk analysis. To put this in some perspective, your odds of winning the grand prize in the Powerball Lottery are 1 in 175,223,510. That would definitely place it in the lowest of the Extremely Low category. Most of the major disasters we've considered are anywhere from hundreds to thousands of times more likely. Have you ever played the lottery? Do you want to gamble against something so much more likely to happen?

Some very interesting disaster statistics are available online at www.preventionweb.net, and are given by country. They have breakdowns by fatalities, number of people affected, and economic impact. I recommend looking at your country's statistics before finalizing your risk probabilities.

## Combining Risks and Impacts

Once you categorize the risks of your disasters, you can use them to go back and assign a risk to each impact scenario. Then, the highest risk factor is the minimum one you assign to the impact. For example, if you live in a coastal area prone to earthquakes and determine that the risk of a hurricane in the 1-3 categories is low while the risk of an earthquake in the 4-6 magnitudes is moderate, the risk factor for impacts that would occur as a result of both would be moderate.

In some cases, you might feel that many low risk disasters with the same impact should bump the risk of that impact occurring up to a moderate risk. While that is valid, you can't take twenty disasters with 5% chance of happening and have a 100% chance of that failure. You can't just add up your risks to give a total risk. I've included a short probability primer in Appendix 2 for those whose jobs rarely involve probability theory or it's been a while since your probability and statistics course. It should aid in avoiding the most common pitfalls of both underestimating and overestimating probabilities for multiple events.

## The Human Element

This brings up a practical point of the human element of contingency planning. Sitting in meetings making plans for disaster impacts can be depressing. After all, you end up talking about massive destruction and possible deaths in terms that hit very close to home. It's a good idea to plan something entirely different to lighten the mood after a run of these meetings. Although this chapter is on risk analysis, the same goes for the subsequent chapter planning meetings whenever they deal with facing the stark realities of catastrophic disasters.

Another thing to realize is that, by having prepared for various disasters, you may actually save lives after a disaster. Having food and water on hand for disasters is just one way your company's preparedness can help your employees. You may want to consider having a company-wide disaster preparedness seminar where home preparedness education is given for the same disasters for which you've prepared your business. Many emergency organizations have brochures which can be made available to your employees to take home from seminars. If you need a business case for this other than goodwill, remember that the employees best able to take care of themselves and their families after a disaster are most likely to be available to implement your business disaster plans.

## Example Risk Analysis

Let's take an example to show how all this works. I'm going to pick a site in Memphis, Tennessee, as my place of business. This is just an example, however; I make no warranty as to the accuracy of the risk levels I'm assigning. In fact, some of these change significantly in different parts of Memphis (flooding recurs near some of the rivers and creeks).

### Table of Risks

First, we want to make our table of risks, which starts on the next page. We'll go down our list. I'm including an explanation of each risk factor; you may want to include that with yours as well. That way, you'll have an idea why you chose that risk level for that disaster type. You'll also notice that I broke up some of them into multiple categories for reasons that will be obvious when reading the chart.

| Disaster | Estimated Risk | Explanation |
| --- | --- | --- |
| Fire (Localized) | Moderate | Fire in datacenter moderate risk with equipment – faulty electronics can start electrical fires |
| Flooding (Basements) | Moderate | Happens during heavy rains |
| Flooding (Plumbing) | Moderate | If you have restrooms, there's always a risk |
| Flooding (Other) | Extremely Low | Site not near rivers or drainage |
| Tornado/High Winds | Moderate | Tornado-prone area |
| Lightning Strikes | Low | Happen often; seldom strike buildings |
| Hurricane/Typhoon /Cyclone | Extremely Low | Non-coastal [no need to split into categories 1-3 and 4-5 when it doesn't apply] |
| Earthquake 5-6M | Low | New Madrid seismic zone |
| Earthquake 7-8M | Very Low | 600-year frequency on 1811-1812 quakes estimated from native American lore |
| Mudslide/Landslide /Avalanche/ Sinkhole | Extremely Low | Except as earthquake result |
| Tsunami/ Tidal Waves | Extremely Low | Non-coastal |
| Volcanic Eruption | Extremely Low | No nearby volcanoes |
| Extremes of Unusual Heat/Cold | Moderate | Ice storms and summer heat |
| Biological Plagues/Epidemics/ Pandemics | Low | Hoping this remains low; the Ebola outbreaks just months ago caused international alarm |
| Solar Flares/ Electromagnetic Pulse | Very Low | Solar flares happen, but chance of impact is very low |
| Power Outages (Short-Term) | High | Common to lose power multiple times a year |
| Power Outages (Days) | Moderate | Ice storms and high winds major contributors |
| Power Outages (Weeks) | Very Low | Occasionally days stretch to a week or more |

| Disaster | Estimated Risk | Explanation |
|---|---|---|
| Hacking – Data Theft | Moderate | Be prepared. |
| Hacking – Data Manipulation or Deletion | Moderate | Be prepared. |
| Hacking – Service Disruption | Moderate | Be prepared. |
| Human Error – Data Loss and/or Service Disruption | Moderate | Be prepared. |
| Cloud Provider/ Outsourcer Failure – Short Term | High | Most of our cloud services experience multiple outages over the course of a year |
| Cloud Provider/ Outsourcer Failure – Long Term | Very Low | May need to break this down by provider in the future |
| Accidents – Road, Rail, Air (Plane), Water (Barge/Ship) | Very Low | Transmodal transportation area - barges, trucks, railroad, and major air cargo hub |
| Structural Failures – Buildings, Dams, Bridges, etc. | Very Low | Bridges in area over rivers have major impact on transportation |
| Terrorism, Riots, and Warfare | Very Low | Ferguson, MO, shows what can happen |

## Table of Risk Impacts

Next, we take the previous table, remove the Extremely Low risks, and use the third column to list possible impacts of these disasters.

| Disaster | Estimated Risk | Possible Impacts |
|---|---|---|
| Fire (Localized) | Moderate | Anywhere from likely minor damage to unlikely building(s) destroyed |
| Flooding (Basements) | Moderate | Things in basements on floor will suffer water damage |
| Flooding (Plumbing) | Moderate | Almost any area can receive water damage from overhead pipes or floor flooding |
| Tornado/High Winds | Moderate | Trees down, power loss, buildings damaged |
| Lightning Strikes | Low | Power surge, equipment damage, fire |
| Earthquake 5-6M | Low | Structural damage to buildings, roads, and bridges, gas and water line ruptures, possible raised floor collapses in datacenters, power outages |
| Earthquake 7-8M | Very Low | Most buildings destroyed, transportation disrupted, major damage to power, water, and gas lines; death, injuries, and destruction widespread |
| Extremes of Unusual Heat/Cold | Moderate | Both frequent and extended power outages, danger of exposure to weather |
| Biological Plagues/ Epidemics/ Pandemics | Low | Sickness and death, quarantines (stay home), hospitals overloaded |
| Solar Flares/ Electromagnetic Pulse | Very Low | Possible computer errors and data loss; more severe if EMP – mass equipment failures |
| Power Outages (Short-Term) | High | Power loss and possible equipment damage |
| Power Outages (Days) | Moderate | Power loss with extended outage to HVAC; beyond UPS capacity to maintain power |
| Power Outages (Weeks) | Very Low | Same as above but possible generator refueling problems |
| Hacking – Data Theft | Moderate | Servers may need to be taken offline for forensics and remediation (rebuild) |

| Disaster | Estimated Risk | Explanation |
|---|---|---|
| Hacking – Data Manipulation or Deletion | Moderate | Servers will need to be taken offline for forensics and remediation (rebuild and restore last known good data) |
| Hacking – Service Disruption | Moderate | Mitigation steps taken may require service changes. |
| Human Error – Data Loss and/or Service Disruption | Moderate | Upgrades gone wrong or files or data deleted in error; many possible impacts and as many options to repair |
| Cloud Provider/ Outsourcer Failure – Short Term | High | Service unavailable; must communicate with vendor and user community |
| Cloud Provider/ Outsourcer Failure – Long Term | Very Low | Service unavailable; recovery plan needed to resume service |
| Accidents – Road, Rail, Air (Plane), Water (Barge/Ship) | Very Low | Possible evacuation due to hazardous materials, physical damages near accident (people and things), transportation impaired |
| Structural Failures – Buildings, Dams, Bridges, etc. | Very Low | Bridge outages would impair transportation |
| Terrorism, Riots, and Warfare | Very Low | Personal safety issues, destruction of property |

As you can see from the chart, damage to buildings can occur with many of the disasters. You can't afford to assume that the building housing your datacenter won't be affected.

The last step in risk analysis deals with that impact column. You may, for clarity's sake, like to create another table where you reverse the columns, showcasing the impacts and combining disasters with like impacts in the third column, repeating them as necessary. You will have to assume certain losses in the impacts to pull all the possible contributing disasters together.

Once you take a particular service and are looking at it from that perspective, it becomes obvious from the business impact analysis which one of the impacts from the risks tables will affect you. Just go down the chart of impacts. For many services, all of the possible impacts could affect the service. The least obvious is the human factor, because you probably didn't specify the staffing required to provide each service. In scenarios where sickness, injury, or deaths are involved, you have to consider those impacts.

# Chapter 4: <u>Risk Avoidance and Mitigation</u>

Perhaps the best avenue of contingency planning is to avoid the disaster in the first place. At this stage, you want to look at the risks from your risk analysis and see if there is a way either to avoid it or do something to minimize the effects. The "best disaster" is one that you avoid entirely. As Benjamin Franklin said, "An ounce of prevention is worth a pound of cure."

For a mitigation example, take the case of a datacenter fire. You can't rule one out, but having a fire suppression system in place with a clean agent halocarbon gas that won't harm the equipment is a great way to stop the fire from spreading from one rack to another. Dealing with a destroyed rack of equipment is much better than recovering from a charred datacenter.

For the hacking list of disasters, continuously improving security to the point that you aren't as attractive a target to outside hackers and have procedures in place to minimize hacking opportunities from insiders is far better than dealing with the aftermath.

Most of you have already mitigated the effect of power outages with uninterruptible power systems (UPS), possibly backed by generators for longer duration power losses. Since the risk of short-term loss of power is almost certain, you've more than likely already addressed that issue. If not, the path ahead should be fairly clear as to how to address it. If you're in an area where rolling blackouts are the norm, you get to test your backup power on a regular basis. You just need to consider the options for outages of longer durations.

For risk avoidance, moving your datacenter from an area on a hundred-year flood plain to a hilltop on a ten-thousand year flood plain is going to reduce the risk of river or flash flooding disasters to near zero. That's probably not something you'd do lightly, but if you're building a new datacenter, why not investigate other sites? Making sure that pipe endings near or over your datacenter are not just shut off at a valve but also capped is another avoidance technique for water damage. It's inexpensive but can prevent major damage.

One thing all of these avoidance and mitigation examples have in common is this: you have to do it ahead of a disaster. Sometimes the costs of avoidance or mitigation changes are minor but have the potential to save a great deal of money when things go wrong. These should be "no-brainers" to decide to implement. But, if you don't spend time thinking about them ahead of time, you'll have major regrets when something does happen that you could have easily avoided.

Sometimes the costs of avoidance or mitigation are not minor. That's when you have to weigh the probability of the disaster times the cost of the disaster against the cost of the avoidance or mitigation. You might use an equation like this to decide to proceed with your implementation:

(probability * cost-of-disaster) ≥ cost of avoidance or mitigation

The difficult thing about this is, of course, coming up with an accurate probability and disaster cost. The cost of the avoidance or mitigation changes is probably easy to estimate with some quotes.

Just as an example, let's assume you think there's a 1% chance of a fire in your datacenter over its useful life. Adding together the cost of replacing or repairing the building, replacing the equipment, and the lost revenue and personnel time while this is being done, let's say you come up with $20 million. As you can see, there are many factors that come into play estimating the cost of a disaster, and they'll be very business-specific. Anyway, the left side of the equation becomes $200,000; if the total cost of a fire suppression system is less than that, you should get one. I'm pulling these numbers out of the air – they're not supposed to accurately reflect anyone's real-life business. If you don't have off-site backups or a mirror site, **the cost on the left side of the equation could be your business**.

You may also want to factor in insurance. Perhaps the building and equipment would be covered by fire insurance. However, many insurance companies will give you a discount on your policy if you have an automatic fire suppression system installed, so that savings should be factored in as well.

In summary, you can see that decisions as to what to do to avoid or mitigate disasters are less straight-forward once you get past simple and inexpensive things. You may also want to re-visit this plan once you work through your business continuity and disaster recovery sections, as they will help you solidify what's really involved.

# Chapter 5:
# Business Continuity Plan

Business continuity planning (BCP) is all about how to keep your business running between the time a disaster occurs and when you've recovered from it. The scenarios are the same ones you'll use later for your disaster recovery planning, but the focus here is more immediate.

There are two common scopes for business continuity plans. The first is just to cover what to do until your disaster recovery plan provides support (between the disaster and your recovery time objective). The second adds detail as to what to do during the disaster recovery plan period until services are restored back to normal. Which path you take will depend on how business-oriented your disaster recovery plan is covering the time period it's in place. You can omit the second part if it's already included in your disaster recovery plan.

Another area you should consider incorporating for your business continuity plan is the "Biological Plagues, Epidemics, Pandemics" response. Personnel are affected, but most of your usual disaster recovery options will not be needed. If the service can easily be provided while working from home, you may not need much of a plan if you already allow occasional remote work. If the service normally utilizes face-to-face human interaction but does not actually require it, you should consider the best options for substitutes. Technology is well positioned in many areas to provide other options, allowing things like banking or video conferencing via mobile applications or computers in homes. Physical presence is often not required. Healthcare is an obvious exception, though consulting physicians may be connected remotely as is being done with greater and greater frequency (especially in areas where specialists are not available).

## Business Continuity Internal Constraints

One thing that is different about the time between the disaster and when the disaster recovery services become active is the availability of IT staff resources. When making your business continuity plans, you should assume that IT staff resources will also be unavailable. Most of them are going to be hard at work on the disaster recovery priorities. It will certainly absorb your infrastructure and applications groups. The one area you may still be able to call on is your help desk support, though it is probable that they will be involved in the disaster communications side of things. Once the plans are in place, review both your business continuity and disaster recovery plans to make sure you haven't double-committed your employee resources.

As a general scenario, assume all equipment is gone and you need to find a way to still stay in business. It's here that you'll have to be the most imaginative in your planning.

Perhaps you could purchase laptops, load them with stock software, and still accomplish a service? You'd need to find a way to transfer the data over to your regular system once it's available. Or perhaps good old pen and paper will do for this? That's fast, though there'd be a lot of data entry to be done once the system is back up. Or maybe there's no way on earth this particular service can be provided without your own software and data? If it's a critical service, you have to make sure there is no gap in recovery and if not, that you can just do without it until the recovery is completed.

There are a couple of reasons that it's important to go through the business continuity scenarios and not just rely on your disaster recovery plan:

1. You have the luxury of time to brainstorm various options and think them through. After a disaster, there will be a lot of pressure and little time. You'll come up with much better options by thinking ahead.

2. Some of your best options may require additional work. In the example above in which you use some off-the-shelf software, you can go ahead and try it. You can also write the programs to convert and load the data into either your recovery system (once that's running) or your regular software rather than waiting until the need arises to get it done under a lot of pressure.

If you're not familiar with brainstorming sessions, you let people blurt out whatever comes to mind as a possibility. They don't have to be well-reasoned at all. Then, you come back around and reason them out – you'll probably be able to eliminate 90% of the suggestions as having obvious flaws. But, that other 10% may contain something that you might not have considered but turns out to be an ingenious way to handle the service during the crisis.

If your business is fortunate to have very experienced people, then you may have the advantage of folks who remember how something was done before it was automated by computers. This could be a great start on developing a business continuity plan for those services. If you don't have folks around who can remember how things were done before they were computerized, you can still research this and update it. You don't have to stick with pen and paper – you might incorporate home computers, laptops, tablets, and phablets in your planning. Just make sure they're not depending on any central infrastructure to get whatever work you have for them done.

## External Infrastructure Loss Contingencies

As we saw in our risk assessment, some disasters are very localized while others cover at least the surrounding area. If you're planning for the latter case, you should assume that cellular networks in that surrounding area are out of commission, too. Satellite phones[8] and amateur (a.k.a. ham) radios are often the only remaining communication methods after hurricanes and earthquakes. So, if you're planning on everyone using their mobile phone to communicate because the land lines are down, you'll probably be out of touch for some time. If you do opt for satellite phones, make sure you have a procedure for their location and routine testing. Having employees issued one keep it at home until an emergency may be your best plan, with monthly tests and recommendations for keeping them charged.

The same goes for wireless data networks. Mass purchases of cellular data wireless hotspots to replace missing network infrastructure may not help you at all in such an emergency. However, there are satellite hotspot devices available. You'll want to test how well these work and keep them in a secure nearby offsite location; you don't want them in the same place you're recovering from a localized disaster, but close enough that you can retrieve them quickly and put them into use. If you have contingency office space for disaster recovery, that would be the logical location.

Basic utilities such as power and water can be out for extended periods after large-scale disasters such as earthquakes and hurricanes, too. Even if your structure is intact and you have generator power, what will you do without water and basic sanitation? You may still be shut down because of something as simple as no restroom facilities. Perhaps your business continuity plan could include bottled water and chemical toilets if you need personnel on site?

When it comes to testing your business continuity plan, it should be done as part of your disaster recovery testing wherever feasible. Since I'm going to go into a lot of detail later in the disaster recovery chapter about testing, I'm not going to repeat it here.

## Example Business Continuity Plan

Now we refer back to our payroll service example that we specified in our business impact analysis.

We're not going to put in anything special for working remotely in case of a biological disaster since we normally allow our staff to work from home on occasion using their business laptops and this service doesn't require any face-to-face interaction.

| Business Continuity Plan | |
|---|---|
| Service | Payroll |
| Description | The payroll service consists of time and leave entry, all deductions and bonuses, and bank transmissions for employee pay. |
| Responsible Party | Shelia Gallivant Compensation Director, HR |
| Plan for Continuing Business | After loss of Base ERP HR System, contact MyBank and inform them to re-use our last payroll ACH transmission. We will not have a continuity process for time and leave entry. We will reconcile payroll changes once time and leave reporting are available again within the ERP HR System. |
| Testing Plan | 1. Call and verify that our business continuity agreement is still valid for running our payroll with the last valid transmitted file. 2. Create deposit corrections as if last month's file was sent for this month, but do not transmit. 3. Verify checks could be printed manually for new employees. |

We've set up an agreement with MyBank that they will retain our payroll transmission files for the last month and can re-use them in case of an outage of our payroll system. New employees will have to be handled manually and employees who no longer work here may get an extra deposit for the extra payroll, which will have to be corrected. Differences in bonus pay will be made up by deposit corrections where in the employee's favor or corrected in the next check if they were paid too much; we don't want to remove funds already paid in that case and will also send a letter to that effect with the amount being withheld from the next check.

Now, it's possible that some service other than payroll may have a more immediate need for the Base ERP HR System, and we may not have to use our continuity plan because the system will not be out long. However, we still may want to re-use the last payroll if the disaster prevented employees from being able to enter their time and leave information for the current pay period, even if the system to generate the payroll file is available.

# Chapter 6:
# Disaster Recovery Plan

At last, we come to the chapter that motivated many of you to read a book on disaster preparedness. If you're reading this chapter and don't have any of the other plans in the works, don't despair. I'm going to share one of my experiences with you. It will also demonstrate why I spent so much time in the first chapter on executive support.

I was the project lead for a contingency planning project. I had an associate vice-president and a couple of directors from the IT division on my team. I was assured we had the executive support we needed. We did a lot of research in the best way to proceed. We went through the planning for a business impact analysis, developed a web-based application for it with database storage. Our CIO reviewed it and made recommendations for changes. Those were made, and we were ready to go. And it went... absolutely nowhere.

You see, our chief financial officer (CFO) went to a conference where everyone was talking about disaster preparedness for the avian flu. It's the one disaster scenario, pandemic/epidemic, that assumes no equipment, data, or service loss. Our CFO wanted this instead of our contingency planning efforts. I was not privy to discussions between our CIO and CFO to know why the smaller scope was chosen, but that's what our business proceeded to do.

What we ended up with was of little help in planning for other disasters. They didn't even make reduced staffing assumptions for sickness and death due to the pandemic. The end product was a great work-from-home plan and how to provide services to clients from their homes. All this would help prevent the spread of the flu in the event of a pandemic. What we *should* have had would have included that as just one piece of our disaster preparedness plans.

So, what did we do? After unsuccessfully attempting to restart the process, we decided to pick some centrally-supported services that we knew needed protection. Our network director arranged for racks and network access in a datacenter a couple-hundred miles away. As a part of this, we also identified other services that we knew had no disaster plans and made sure that our CIO had this list to present to the executive committee, to get support and funding for adding more services to our disaster site preparations. We gradually added onto the list of services, and I understand that continued after I left. Am I confident that they'll be in good shape after a disaster? No, I don't believe they will have everything covered as needed without good data from a business impact analysis. But, I am confident that they'll be in *much* better shape than if we'd let the failure to do proper planning stop us.

Something is better than nothing. If you reach this point and don't have the business support you need to do it right, **do the best you can with what resources you have. It may still be enough to save your business.**

## Hot Sites, Warm Sites, and Cold Sites
No discussion of disaster recovery would be complete without talking about other sites that could host your services. A **hot site** is one that is running the same software that the datacenter you're recovering is running. You might have the current load balanced between the two sites in an active-active scenario. ("Active-active" is just what you think – both sites services are active at the same time.) In an active-passive scenario, the applications are running and data is synchronized, but the "passive" side is just waiting to become active. There are some applications that don't work well with the latency between the datacenters or being on a different network, so active-passive is the best you can do. A hot site active-passive switch to passive-active is assumed to be quick and

automatic.  If it's not, it's considered a **warm site**, which is one that is ready and waiting for certain manual steps to be performed but can be up and running in a matter of minutes instead of seconds.  The equipment costs of hot and warm sites are similar; it's the disaster recovery steps that really distinguish between the two and the application designs that dictate which one to use.

So, what's a **cold site**?  It's one that has some hardware standing by but will likely need to have data restored there and some configuration work done before becoming operational.  Often, backup data is replicated to the site, which is much simpler than dealing with logical disks in a physical server environment. The recovery time objective for a cold site is typically hours or days, depending on the setup.  Still, it's way ahead of not having something ready to use.  Preparing datacenter space and ordering equipment, even if prioritized shipments are guaranteed, would take weeks.  It would also take time to find a cloud vendor and create a solution there.  However, you can consider a cloud hot, warm, or cold site ahead of time and work that into your plan.

**Despite the terminology, hot, warm, and cold sites are really application or service-specific.**  For example, most folks running cold sites for services have at least their Internet domain name server (DNS) [translates internet host names to their internet addresses] running active at the cold site by having a secondary name server running there; for DNS services, it's a hot site.  It's also not unusual to have some hardware available for BIA tier three or four services as a cold site for services at your "hot site" datacenter for prolonged outages.  To further confuse matters, multiple-datacenter setups within companies commonly are set up to be each other's recovery sites: hot, warm, and cold.

One important factor when choosing a location or vendor for a remote site is "Are they going to be impacted by the same disaster?"  If the answer is "yes" in some scenarios, perhaps you need a site a bit farther away.  On the other hand, you don't necessarily want to choose the farthest away that you can; network issues such as increased latency and available bandwidth will limit your recovery options. So, if you're using a cloud provider for your remote site, it's still important to know the locations of which datacenters that will be hosting your services. If your services will be running actively in multiple cloud datacenters, you may get the best of both worlds by doing your normal communications with one nearby and yet have the availability of one that is more remote.

Let's suppose for a bit that your company in the United States has offices with datacenters in New York, Chicago, Dallas, and Los Angeles. If I were going to pair them up for disaster recovery sites, I'd probably pair New York with Dallas and Los Angeles with Chicago. Why? New York and Chicago could suffer from the same extreme cold system. The distance from New York to Los Angeles is less than ideal. So, New York gets Dallas as the preferred replication site. Each of the pairings is geographically diverse enough not to be caught up in the same disaster (unless it's a national one such as war) while being closer than coast-to-coast. It's possible that you could make all four datacenters replicas of each other if you have the money and business case for it, which would be even better from a disaster recovery standpoint.

## Impact Analysis Revisions Due to "Budget Veto"
Unless you've really stressed the importance of not placing services at too high a criticality or too low recovery time, things may change once you get a price tag. If the cost for providing what was specified is higher than management is willing to pay, their view of how critical it really is to get running within that time may undergo some adjustment.

If the user of the service is already paying for it and will also incur the cost of recovery initiatives, it's somewhat self-policing. If the service is in some overhead charges, though, and the recovery is also going to be thrown in there, it's going to take more discussion to keep the budget in line. If it's important enough to the business, it's important enough to budget. **After all, the cost of**

**not preparing ahead of a disaster will often dwarf the cost of being prepared.** Many times, it will determine whether you stay in business after a disaster, too.

The people who won't think that the money spent being prepared for disasters isn't well spent are those who don't think you'll have any such disasters. Whether you're willing to gamble your business on being disaster-free for any major disasters is an upper-level management decision, though don't forget legal and regulatory requirements still must be satisfied, regardless.

## Benefits and Risks of Disaster Recovery Services

There are some advantages to using a company that is in the business of providing disaster recovery services. We covered a little of it in the business impact analysis chapter, namely that they can guide you through the contingency planning process and have some DR product offerings. It's a "buyer-beware" market, though.

Let's take a major but not catastrophic earthquake example. Roads with bridges and overpasses, phone lines, and power lines are out of commission. How are companies that promise mobile office space and datacenter setups going to deliver them? If the company is a smaller local one and their "office on wheels" survives, how many other companies in the area did they promote this solution for? Who actually gets to have it? You're likely better off with a remote site solution for this level of disaster.

## Developing the Plan

So, we've got a list of services. We know how long we can be without each of them, how current the data must be for those that are data-based, and what capacity we need to provide until such time as original or replacement service is restored. Each of them needs a plan for recovering from an outage. There are also three sub-plans that every DR plan needs to have, which we'll cover in detail. In some ways, a part of our work is done for us with our BIA because the objectives for recovery time, data point recovery, and capacity will determine what our options are.

## Data Security

It's important when developing your DR strategies to keep data security in mind. If your DR plan puts your data at increased risk, your business needs to decide if that risk is acceptable. I stress this because some "easy and cheap" options that could work for recovery may not meet your existing security policies. I'm not saying that you shouldn't accept some increased risks, only that you should go into this with your eyes wide open to them. You don't want to cause one disaster by planning to recover from another one.

There are a few ways to reduce your risks. One is by keeping the data under your own control in your own datacenters. Another is to make sure it's encrypted in transit between servers and at rest on disk, only being decrypted in memory when in use. Another is to use test data for all your testing and only use real data in the event of an actual disaster. These all have their drawbacks. If you don't already have multiple datacenters, the first option is very expensive. The second option, encryption, adds to the workload on the equipment and the complexity of the setup. It may not be supported by the software in use, either. The third option, test data, may not give as good a test as the real data and isn't practical in hot or warm site setups.

I'm going to be giving lots of options in the following section that have various security implications. Remember to evaluate the options based on your own security requirements. It would be very tedious if I kept repeating the same security concerns with each option with "if you're currently doing this list of things, then that adds these risks". Your security review is implied for all options.

## Deciding on Off-Site Options

Any service that needs a recovery time objective (RTO) in the range of a few seconds is going to require a hot site. Any service that needs data current within a few seconds (RPO) is going to require data replication to that site. When getting estimates of what this will actually take, you might be surprised by the expense. Double the original cost in addition is not uncommon. Yes, you're basically doubling the hardware and software (though many software vendors will let you run DR copies with no fees). The rest of the cost comes from getting the replication going. You'll either need licenses for storage systems to replicate if they support it or purchase appliances to do the work at both sites. Another piece of this is the network bandwidth and point-to-point encryption you'll want to use if sending the data over the Internet (still less expensive than leasing a direct line in most cases).

One way to keep costs in line for warm or cold sites is to see if cloud offerings will work. You could keep a minimal service presence running at your recovery cloud site that could have more servers added if you actually needed to use the site for your service. In cloud computing parlance, the dynamic addition of resources is known as "cloud bursting". You need to have the data there in some form (periodic copies or replication). This would work whether you are coming from a datacenter or another cloud vendor.

The least expensive off-site option is one where you have no equipment, but store recent copies of your backup tapes off-site. Companies such as Iron Mountain are in the business of picking up your tapes, storing them indexed in a vault, and returning them or delivering them to an alternate location in case of disaster. That location could be a cold site, or it could just be a place where you'll have replacement hardware delivered as well, depending on your needs. Or, if you really want to insure your data survives, you have both offsite tapes and backups replicated to a cold site. That's the option I chose the last time I set up a cold site. If you're concerned about the safety of your data, there are backup software options that will encrypt the tapes – just make sure you've been equally careful to preserve the decryption key from a disaster. Loss of the decryption key renders your backups useless, which is only what you want them to be for someone else trying to read them!

**Research, Planning Sessions, and Implementation**
At this point, your infrastructure and applications support folks are going to be spending a lot of time planning how to provide the level of service you've determined in your BIA in regards to your recovery objectives. I'm going to go into some of the things that they'll need to consider, but it's a major section of "Geek Speak". Readers who want to skip this next section can flip over to page 63 where we begin discussion on the actual plans.

 Warning!
Geek
Speak

*Data*
In addition to the type of disaster recovery site that will be needed, you've got to figure out how it'll actually work. **Data replication is typically the major issue in providing recovery point objectives (RPO).** You'll have to determine whether you're going to depend on a combination of storage area network (SAN) controller replication of disk images, database-level replication, or file-level synchronization methods.

Even within those, most SAN replication can be done synchronously or asynchronously. Synchronous replication means that the I/O doesn't complete until the data is replicated and is only feasible in low-latency situations. Asynchronous replication lets the I/O complete and then replicates the data to the target system. At any given time, the replica copy could be a little behind updates of the original data.

While synchronous replication guarantees the data is identical, you'll have to locate the replica SAN near enough by that you can always get quick response times. The upper limit distance-wise is typically given as 100km (62 miles) as the wires or fiber optics run. In practice, however, it's something considerably less than that geographically, typically 40km (25 miles) is reasonable. That's far enough away for some disasters, but not wide-area effect ones (such as earthquakes and hurricanes). Since the I/O is waiting on the remote site response, you will have a slower response time for your local SAN, too.

In addition, there are various appliances that work with SAN controllers to provide replication. One such appliance claims to allow up to 50ms response times for synchronous replication in some applications up to 2,000 miles (3,200km) away. Single-digit millisecond response times are typically required for successful synchronous replication, so this is quite a departure from normal requirements. That's one of which I'd want to test a demo unit before buying.

Another data replication consideration is how to limit the amount of data needing to be sent to reduce bandwidth requirements. Any time your data volume exceeds your bandwidth, latency skyrockets as data has to be cached (ideally) or retransmitted (even worse). **Data deduplication and compression options rank high on reducing the bandwidth demands.**

In general, synchronous replication either requires a direct link or a guaranteed quality of service (QoS) from a shared network provider. It is very latency-sensitive, so occasional bandwidth saturation isn't acceptable. More on networking very shortly.

Things get more complex when you bring in cloud services. I don't know of a way to do synchronous data replication between cloud providers. You might even have to use a fallback position of having a server there with access to the data ship it over to a server at the other provider who can store it. While cloud providers are usually good at replicating data within their cloud, their marks go down replicating outside it. There aren't currently any standards for replication between clouds. Unfortunately, many of the historic cloud outages have not been successful at maintaining availability even with multiple sites. Sometimes, it's been the data replication software itself that's been at fault, making the data equally unavailable at all of their sites.

## Networks

Providing multiple paths via multiple providers to your networks requires more research. You have to use the BGP protocol if there are multiple paths to your IP network from the Internet. You will have to decide if you also want multiple paths to your remote site.

Normally, a remote site would imply a different IP network or subnet as well. Some options are available using protocols like MPLS to make your remote site seem like an extension of your local site, effectively tunneling through your provider's network. Since MPLS can do quality-of-service (QoS) and tunnel layer 2 or 3 protocols, you have a lot of options there for virtual private local area networks (LAN) or wide area networks (WAN). Layer 2 makes more sense if you have multiple small sites around town – the latency on long distance connections makes layer 3 preferable.

I've already mentioned in passing that you'd want an active DNS server at your remote sites. If you're using BIND software, you'd need to be prepared to make the remote site secondary DNS the primary one so changes could be made. If you're using appliances like Infoblox, you may have other options rather than the traditional primary/secondary DNS setup. Odds are good that there are several DNS records that will need to be updated in the event of a site failover. Use of appliances such as global site selectors can handle hot site requirements, but services that are warm or cold site setups may at least require a CNAME record change to refer to a server at the recovery site. You'll want to pay special attention to the time-to-live (TTL) set on these records, as that should[9] determine how long other, non-authoritative DNS servers cache the information without asking your servers again.

## Servers and Storage

If you're considering cloud options, you don't really care what the equipment is on the other side, only its compatibility and performance characteristics. If you're planning on your own remote datacenter, then you have a lot of options.

If you've still got some proprietary UNIX systems, you'll need hardware that can run them. I do not recommend using Linux at the remote site and UNIX on your regular systems. There's too much opportunity for things to go wrong. If you've got your application running on Linux, then use that everywhere. If your budget is tight, put your older systems at your recovery site whenever they're replaced at your regular site (the hardware lifecycle for most proprietary UNIX hardware is about seven years – maybe years eight through ten could be at your recovery site, keeping some extras of each type there to either swap or use for spare parts). It may not be ideal, but you'll be thankful for anything that works in a disaster situation.

Depending on your recovery capacity objective (RCO), you might also get by with less capable equipment at your recovery site. Servers that are slower or a smaller virtual environment may be adequate. Maybe a less expensive SAN will work there, too. With the SAN, you just need to make sure that whatever replication you need is still supported. If you're using appliances for the replication, you may be able to get away with more diversity there.

If you're running active-passive hot site recovery, you also have the option of putting the newer equipment at your recovery site and making it the active site. Whenever you need to upgrade hardware, you can save on downtime by upgrading the passive site and making it active afterwards.

If you've successfully implemented a hybrid cloud, where you can run servers and services in your datacenter cloud or a provider's cloud, you also have some more options. You might consider making the provider cloud active and enjoy more features like cloud-bursting, where sudden increases in demand can automatically scale up beyond your local datacenter hardware capacity.

One last issue that's worth mentioning is the situation in which you believe your servers have been hacked. Your computer security incident response team (most organizations of any size have them) should have procedures in place that would eliminate the need for specifically addressing this in your disaster recovery plans. If your recovery servers aren't compromised, you may still implement your disaster recovery plan (or business continuity plan) while the forensics analysis and server rebuilds are being done in your production environment. The proper procedures for handling security incidents is beyond the scope of this book, but you may well find that your disaster recovery planning saves you a lot of downtime from these incidents. If you believe that your recovery servers may be just as vulnerable to the attack used, you will want to secure them before bringing them into service, even if some downtime is involved.

### *Cloudy Services*

While infrastructure-level cloud services can usually be duplicated elsewhere, you are at a disadvantage when it comes to the upper levels like software as a service (SaaS). Your SaaS vendor may be your only source and recourse. If they offer local software solutions, you can talk to them about options for shipping your data down periodically or replicating it to your site, where you'll have the software setup ready to implement if necessary. They may even give you a break on the licensing for only running for disaster recovery. If they don't offer data transmissions, then you will need to work with them on reviewing *their* disaster recovery procedures to make sure that they can satisfy your needs. You'd still be vulnerable if they went out of business, but you can work at surviving the destruction of *their* datacenter where your application runs.

Most of the larger vendors have multiple datacenters already replicating data. They may charge an additional fee to run your service in multiple datacenters. They may be willing to only charge the fee if the service needs to move. Don't assume that will happen automatically. Also, in cases of outages that are caused by storage system software failures, all datacenters are affected. It's less than ideal to have to depend on your cloud provider's cloud.

Another option that's sometimes available is a third-party data broker. The cloud provider provides access for the data broker to keep copies of your data. This usually means replication where the broker has a datacenter near each of the cloud provider sites. Then, if something happens to the cloud provider, your data is still safe at the broker sites (at least the ones that are remote to the replicating one if it's an area disaster). If you don't have software available to make use of the data, you've got a long road ahead, but at least the data still exists.

### *In Summary*

So, let's say you've spent a few months figuring it all out and another period of time implementing it. You're pretty sure you can meet all your objectives in your BIA (you may have revised the objectives to something you can afford). You've got hot, warm, or cold site services, or forget about the service until things are back to normal (yes, that's an option for some of your minimal impact BIA tier services). You're good to go, right? Nope, you have to detail how to get from "normal" to "disaster recovery mode" and back as well as how you plan to test it all to make sure it'll work.

Returning You to Non-Geek Speak ☺

### Failover Plan

The failover plan is the one you use to migrate failed services over to your recovery solution. When most folks think of a disaster recovery plan, this is the plan that springs to mind. They don't think about all the hard work done previously to prepare to finally make it this far. Remote sites appear effortlessly to those not involved in provisioning them, whether in a vendor cloud, datacenter, or your own remote datacenter. A printed plan of what to do during a disaster is something tangible that they can point to and say "Here's our plan!" So, let's get this plan going.

For each service, every step needed to recover that service needs to be detailed. You should have as few generic steps as possible (avoid directions such as "log on to the computer with your credentials" instead of using the more detailed "on the console of flodb.example.com, enter your username and password"); you want actual system names, commands, mouse clicks, everything every step of the way. Remember, you might not be the one recovering the service, so someone who's never done what you're describing is your target audience.

The more work that is done before a disaster usually means less work after one. If you've got hot site services running, your failover plan is primarily going to be a lot of checking to see if things are still working properly. For warm site services, you'll have each step of how the failover is to be accomplished in addition to how to check to insure it's working correctly. This plan will be more a bit longer. If you have cold site services, the plan will have to include setups, file and data restoration, and a large range of other possible tasks that might include network, DNS, and even personnel changes.

A failover plan is going to be cross-functional. While each team may write their part of the plan, you'll probably need a section for network engineers, systems engineers/administrators, database administrators, application support teams, and, unless the changes are completely transparent for use, the end users. I recommend that each section be maintained by the team that will be doing the work. Wherever something is accomplished and turned over to another team, that must be documented and obvious in both team report sections. The order that things are accomplished is usually critical, and anytime one team has to perform some set of actions and then have another team perform other actions, there should be no stalling of the recovery process from miscommunication. All handoffs of activity should be clearly documented, including how notification of the current status to each team involved is performed.

## Failback Plan

The failback plan is the one you'll use to migrate services from your recovery solution back to their original state. It's easy to make the mistake of thinking you'll just reverse the failover process to fail back. However, in many cases, failing back may be harder than the failing over in the first place. For example, some site recovery tools have a software switch you can flip to automate the failover, but you can't just flip it back to accomplish a failback. The failback process is often more manual than the failover. Now, you're probably not under the same time pressures to failback to your original setup, so you can excuse some extra work in the failback.

Be just as detailed in your failback plans as you were in your failover plans. Don't assume someone knows how things were working pre-failover. In other words, don't say "restore the DNS entries to their original values". Either give the values or give the place where you saved them in your failover plan to recover them in this plan.

It's normal to find omissions in your failover plan as you're developing your failback plan. In the previous example, you may realize you need to copy the current state of something before you change it so you can restore it correctly later.

For the most part, anything I mentioned for the failover plan also goes for the failback plan.

## Testing Plan

There are some simple rules to follow for testing plans:

1. **Do no harm.** You don't want your testing to have a negative impact on your production environment.
2. **Use as much of your failover and failback plans as possible** for your testing plan. This is easiest for hot site services and the most difficult for cold site/no site services. Refer to rule 1.

3. **Have people that didn't develop the plans test them.** The best way to make sure things are documented well is have folks who didn't write it test it. If they have to ask someone else for help or clarification, that means updating the documentation with this information.
4. **Review the tests.** For anything that wasn't clear or has changed since the last test, make sure that failover, failback, and testing plans are updated. If you've followed rule 2, most changes necessary for the failover and failback plans will be caught when testing.

It's very important to remember rule 1: Do no harm. If you believe you have hot site services for everything in your datacenter with acceptable recovery objectives, the most realistic test would be to just pull it off the network. If you want to make sure it works at peak times, you could do it at a peak time. However, I'd caution that it would be a very bad idea. You should take a decidedly more conservative approach to your testing.

Expect that there are omissions in your business impact analysis. A more conservative approach of taking down parts of your infrastructure at lower utilization times might make the process of discovering them a gentler experience.

Expect that there are problems with your testing plans (probably some carried over from failover and failback plans). Expecting that you'll get the plans 100% correct on the first take is overly confident. That's why you bother to test the plans – it's to uncover those problems when you have the luxury of things working normally rather than after a disaster.

When documenting the plans, assume that someone with the expertise needed but not the experience at your place of business is doing the recovery. For example, pretend a new hire on your team is going to be following the documents. You don't have to explain concepts but do have to give implementation details. When testing, pick the person with the least knowledge of that service to do the recovery (yes, you can have the person who wrote the documentation watching, but no feedback without changing the documentation to echo the clarification). One hopes that will cover you for the worst-case recovery scenario for your team.

Assume that changes in the environment won't necessarily make it into the plans. For example, I'm going to give my payroll example as is, and after some changes to the process when MyBank is bought up and merged in with MegaBank. The only person the changes affected was the payroll accountant, and she wasn't around when the first plans were made. Her predecessor is now working in a different department. She may remember that plans were documented for disaster recovery, but she doesn't know about the changes.

Obviously, the best test plan would be to mimic the service loss and use your failover and failback plans. You can pretty much do this for hot and warm site services. One of the caveats there is making sure your usage hasn't outstripped the remaining capacity for active-active hot site services. It's easy to experience incremental growth and not realize you're now depending on both sites for the performance you expect.

For hot and warm site services with 100% recovery capacity, I'd recommend doing something like the following in an off-peak month. For each service, on one weekend, failover to your recovery site. Run that week testing to insure all is good. The second weekend, failback to your normal setup. Let everything stabilize again. The third weekend, fail your recovery site – this will impact active-active hot site services. Again, monitor during the following week. The fourth weekend, restore service to your recovery site. You should spend the following week insuring all is normal and then make any updates to plans that became apparent.

For cold site services, your testing plans will likely need to be taking time to bring the services up at your recovery site following your failover plan but not bringing them into production mode. You won't actually be taking down the production side of things because the impact to your services would violate rule 1. You'll want to treat the recovery site like another test environment for the most part. It should mimic your production environment in every way you can accomplish without impacting your production environment. Your testing plan will have to pull out parts of your failover plan to implement, making sure that the parts that would bring it into production are omitted. The failback portion of your testing plan should include the data moves but not the loads back into your production system, for obvious reasons. You'll also need to detail how you plan to test the recovery system for its capabilities to work in the event of a failure of the production system. Having users check it will involve a different set of instructions to access it.

For some services such as e-mail, you might provide another service. For example, if you use Exchange on-site, you could either use Exchange at the recovery site or have plans to provision accounts in Microsoft's Office 365 cloud environment. In either case, users may not have access to their e-mail in their regular mailbox for a period of time as the recovery proceeds but could send and receive e-mails shortly after a disaster. Testing this might involve provisioning the accounts but not changing the mail exchange (MX) records to actually use the alternate e-mail system instead of your usual one.

## Example Disaster Recovery Plans

Now we return to my payroll example for disaster recovery plans. The nitty-gritty highly-detailed plans would be for the "Base ERP HR System." The tedious example would also probably bore everyone, including those normally reading the "Geek Speak" sections. So, my choice of the payroll subsystem will make my example plans mercifully short while still hopefully illustrating the points I'm trying to get across.

Note, I'm also including usernames and passwords in these steps. You should probably have a separate document that is password encrypted to store those and refer to the username but not the password in your main document, referring to the encrypted file.

I'm just further simplifying my example by including them, and they don't actually work anywhere (unless someone unwisely copies them for use after publication).

**Payroll Failover Plan**

1. If the PC with the "MyBank Secure File Transfer" software package is not available, then install the software on another networked PC:
    a. Obtain the software from one of the following:
        i. https://sft.mybank.com
        ii. Copy of install program saved at remote site
    b. Install the software by saving it to the local system, right clicking on the install.exe file, and choose "Run as Administrator"
    c. Accept all the defaults during the installation process
    d. Run the program and select "Edit", and "Account".
    e. Enter "MyBusiness" for the username.
    f. Enter "Iw4nd2c!" for the password. (It's generated from "I wish for no disaster to come!")
    g. Click the "Save" button and close the program.
2. Once the recovery site is available, log into https://erp.example.com, generate the payroll file and save it to the system as usual. [erp.example.com is normally an alias for the canonical name erpprod.example.com, but will be changed to erpdr.example.com as part of the failover process for the ERP system.] If the payroll is not complete, repeat this step once it is for the actual transfer.
3. Verify that time and leave reporting are working and available to employees. If they've been working for long enough to be updated by employees, proceed to step 4. If not, re-use the last payroll as specified in the business continuity plan. This is a management decision.
4. Run the "MyBank Secure File Transfer" program, browsing to the complete payroll file saved in step 2 for the transmission.

**Payroll Failback Plan**

No failback is really necessary. If a new system was setup during failover that will no longer be needed, insure that the payroll files are erased before returning the equipment. We didn't change any time and leave reporting outside the ERP HR System, so the data migrations back will included in the Base ERP HR System plan.

**Payroll Testing Plan**

The testing plan is the same as the failover plan with one exception. We'll use "erpdr.example.com" instead of "erp.example.com" for step 2, since the testing plan for the ERP system does not include replacing the production system and making the change to the "erp.example.com" canonical name alias.

1. For the test, assume the current PC is not available and install "MyBank Secure File Transfer" software package on another networked PC:
   a. Obtain the software from one of the following:
      i. https://sft.mybank.com
      ii. Copy of install program saved at remote site
   b. Install the software by saving it to the local system, right clicking on the install.exe file, and choose "Run as Administrator"
   c. Accept all the defaults during the installation process
   d. Run the program and select "Edit", and "Account".
   e. Enter "MyBusiness" for the username.
   f. Enter "Iw4nd2c!" for the password. (It's generated from "I wish for no disaster to come!")
   g. Click the "Save" button and close the program.
2. Log into https://erpdr.example.com, generate the payroll file and save it to the system as usual.
3. Verify that time and leave reporting are working and available for testing. You must be able to enter data for the payroll period when the simulated disaster started as well as the current pay period.

4. Run the "MyBank Secure File Transfer" program, browsing to the payroll file saved in step 2 for the transmission. Do not actually transmit the file.
5. Erase the payroll files from the test PC and return it.

## Why Tests Need Repeating

Well, that *was* the testing plan. However, when we met with the payroll accountant to run the test, she let us know that MyBank had merged into MegaBank, and MegaBank did not use custom file transfer software. Instead, they had a secure web site that is used to transfer files. In addition, you can check a "test" box when uploading a file that will only upload it and do a file validation check but will not process the file for payroll. It's been working this way the past few months.

So, we have to amend our failover and testing plans with this new information. We delete step 1 and change step 3 to the new directions for the web site instead of PC-based program. Since MegaBank allows testing, in step 3, we'll also add directions to send the file with the "test" box checked and report on file validation success or failure.

**Testing not only does its best to insure the directions are correct, but that they're *still* correct.** How often you execute your tests and for what services is up to you. I recommend testing all services at least once a year and at most once a quarter, unless some automated testing can be accomplished more often.

## Getting Back to Normal

After you've failed over to your recovery site(s) and services are restored, you may have a lot of work ahead before you can execute your failback plan. A lot depends on the condition of your site.

If your buildings were severely damaged or destroyed, you have to decide if you'll set up shop somewhere else or rebuild there. If you're leasing, it's probably going to be quicker to find new space.

If the damage is minor to moderate but the site needs cleanup from water, smoke, or fire damage, there are companies such as ServiceMaster Restore that provide restoration services specializing in making areas inhabitable again after disasters strike. It's more than just a job for mops, buckets, and fans.

It's also an ideal time to consider your mitigation options again. If you're moving or rebuilding, do so with an eye for possible improvements to your disaster risks. Maybe you don't want to be on that thousand-year flood plain after all. Maybe there's land that won't liquefy in the next earthquake (old former landfills are notorious for being unstable, even when the ground isn't shaking).

If rebuilding or major renovations are called for, you also have the opportunity to improve your environmental impact ("go green" with sustainable design) and also save some money on future utility bills. You might also build with an eye to surviving a similar disaster. For example, adding earthquake-resistant features to buildings when they're built is less expensive than repairs or retro-fitting buildings later. Don't depend on widely-varying building codes to enforce sufficient protection.

"Back to normal" may be misleading. Your "new normal" may be very different from the "old normal". While a disaster isn't the reason we'd like for change, take advantage of opportunities for positive changes while trying to preserve the things you value about your organization. The technology or building changes are relatively easy – the most difficult changes may come from missing people who are no longer able to be your coworkers due to injury or death. That is the part of the "new normal" that may take the longest period of adjustment. If that's part of your "new normal", consider making individual and group grief counseling available to your employees.

At the other extreme, if an extended power outage caused you to activate your disaster recovery plan, you may have little to do but bring everything at the old site back online before you can execute your failback plan. That's a much more pleasant scenario.

# Chapter 7:
# Putting the Plans in Place

So, you've developed all the plans in this book. Great! Now what? Well, your work is not quite done yet. You need one more overall plan. It's organizational rather than disaster-specific.

## Declaring a Disaster

The first thing that must be determined is who can declare a disaster and start the other plans in motion? What is the scope of the disaster they are declaring?

Let's say there's a fire in your datacenter. Declare a disaster? No, you need more information. Perhaps the only damage was to a part on the air conditioning unit before the fire burned out. You only need to replace the part (and determine if it was defective or there's a problem with the unit that might cause the replacement to fail in a similar manner). The loss of a single system is probably not a cause to declare a disaster for a service.

Let's say now that the fire took out an entire rack of servers. Once the fire's out and everyone's safe, let's check the scope of the outage. If all the services running on servers in that rack were also being run on servers in other racks, your redundancy (which could have been a part of your disaster mitigation work) has avoided an outage. You'll need to investigate the cause and replace the equipment. You may need to invoke a part of your disaster plan to handle the load or improve redundancy. Even if a service is out, a more limited-in-scope response that quickly restores service may be more appropriate than declaring a disaster for the service.

That gets us back to our question: Who can invoke a disaster recovery plan? By this time, we've seen that our failback plans may be more involved than our failover plans, and neither will be trivial. So, invoking a plan by mistake will cost your business time, possibly money, and may result in diminished capacity for services until the failback is complete. It's not something to be done lightly.

You should identify people in your management structure who understand the implications and are responsible for at least a portion of the services. You might create a hierarchy for it or allow any one of them to do it. For example, maybe you want your CIO to make the call (or the appropriate chief officer for non-IT services). If he's not available, then one of his associates, on down to the directors over the areas involved. Maybe you think any of them should be able to make the call without a hierarchy. This has to be a business decision.

Another issue is the scope of a disaster declaration. Some businesses keep things simple with an all-or-nothing approach. Depending on the size and geographical extent of your resources, this might not make sense for you. Typically, for a small number of service outages, remediation efforts don't require declaring a disaster. If your datacenter is destroyed, that's obviously the time to declare a disaster at least for that entire datacenter. Anything in between is a management call, weighing the appropriateness and effectiveness of invoking your disaster plans versus using normal break-fix methods.

We've also mentioned, in the case of biological disasters, having your business continuity plan for workers and customers to interact remotely. Any face-to-face contact that can be avoided must be avoided in that scenario. Your disaster scope declaration might invoke a business continuity plan for the duration without invoking a disaster recovery plan. The remaining sections apply to both the business continuity plans and the disaster recovery plans, so don't neglect the former when distributing your plans.

## Disaster Communications

Okay, so you know who can start the plans in motion, now what? That's where the disaster communication tree kicks in. Everyone must be told of the disaster (and scope) so that they can do their part. You should have a list of who is responsible for communicating with whom. It's usually simplest if it's organizationally driven. For example, the CIO is responsible for communicating with the other top executives and his direct reports (whether he or an assistant does it). They, in turn, are likewise responsible for communicating with all their direct reports. The other executives are responsible for having someone contact the folks that report under them.

You should gather the following information on all employees and have a copy as part of your communication plan: name, phone numbers (business, mobile, and home), e-mail addresses (business and at least one personal one), their office address and home address. If your business e-mail is down, you might need to use their personal e-mail for a while. If all this information is kept in an HR database, a report needs to be generated and updated in the plan whenever significant changes occur and at least annually.

Since the most important thing after declaring a disaster and scope is communicating that, it must be part of your overall contingency plan.

## Locating the Plans

Once you've got all your plans together with the previous information as the first section, what do you do with them? The answer lies in not solely relying on any of the infrastructure that you're trying to recover.

When I led the IT department at a technical college, I made sure that each manager kept a printed copy of the plan in their homes as well as in their offices. What good is the plan if you can't get to it after a disaster?

Parts of your plan may be digital, such as encryption keys and an encrypted password database for your server administration and service accounts. All of your systems administrators should have a copy of this on a flash drive along with an electronic copy of your contingency plans. In practice, it's best to have each person with two drives and update one each month, swapping it with the one they keep with the plan. They can also update the other and keep it with them, but they always want to have at least one available. The encryption password should not be included as part of the plan, though a secure location for it could be mentioned if you want to assume that no one who knows it may survive the disaster and another secure location for the latest flash drive with the data.

In any case, the entire plan should be treated as confidential, even without password credentials listed. There's enough information in the plans to give a hacker valuable insights to your vulnerabilities and capabilities that you don't want common knowledge. If it's going to be accessible on a web site, make sure it requires authentication. Some data vaulting companies offer online space for plans that you want them to use in case of disaster (please deliver such-and-such tapes to this address) and plans internal to your organization. You might want to take advantage of that for a copy of your plan and encrypted authentication information.

In summary, it's a good idea for anyone involved in communicating disaster information or remediating a disaster to have a copy of the plan at home as well as access to a copy at the office. Anyone needing to store encryption keys or credentials (which also should be encrypted) should have a flash drive with the information stored with their plan.

## Policies and Procedures

Before you're ready to call everything done, make sure you implement policies and procedures that will ensure every new service gets added to your business impact analysis and has disaster planning done as an integral part of your implementation.

Likewise, projects that modify existing services should also have a step for their completion that includes updating the disaster planning for them, and, if necessary, the business impact analysis. If hot sites are required for a service, better to budget for that from the beginning of the implementation project rather than come back later asking for more resources to truly complete the project.

Having these policies and procedures approved and implemented is the last important step of your disaster planning. Failure to implement them will pretty much guarantee that your disaster planning will obsolesce quickly. Worse than having no plans, plans which are of no use can lull you into a false sense of security.

If you've neglected this step, the remediation for it is to do a full review of your Business Impact Analysis that's similar to your starting effort. That will point out newer services where you need to develop the other plans. If you've kept up using your testing plans for business continuity and disaster recovery, you should have captured most of the changes to existing services.

Lastly, make sure you celebrate once you've implemented all of this! You deserve it!

# Appendix 1:
# What Does "Five Nines" Mean, Anyway?

When talking about service availability, you'll often hear some number of "nines". Simply put, it's the percentage uptime. "Five nines" is 99.999% availability. "Three nines" is just 99.9% availability. You get the idea. Here's a table to bring it home:

| Annual Uptime | Annual Downtime Allowable |
|---|---|
| 99.999% | 5 minutes, 15.36 seconds |
| 99.99% | 52 minutes, 33.6 seconds |
| 99.9% | 8 hours, 45 minutes, 36 seconds |
| 99% | 3 days, 15 hours, 36 minutes |

As you can see, "five nines" allows just over five minutes downtime over a whole year – quite ambitious for most services. If you have a service running on only one server, you can see how that wouldn't even give you time to keep the server patched with critical security updates. On the other hand, "three nines" is workable for a single-server service; you could reboot once a month and be down for an average of forty minutes each time and still make it. That's assuming you don't have any unplanned downtime.

One way that people make their "nines" stretch farther is only covering "unplanned downtime". That means that any downtime they plan ahead doesn't count. You have to be careful here; one place I read about was down three days and only claimed about an hour of unplanned downtime – because they made a plan about how to restore service and the remainder was therefore "planned downtime"! This is clearly beyond what any reasonable person would count as planned downtime.

Why does this matter? Well, it's a way of measuring availability for service level agreements (SLA). If they're internal to your business, you can generally agree on what types of downtime are covered (everything or just outages outside an agreed upon maintenance window). If you're contracting with a third party, you need to really have the terms spelled out as to what constitutes downtime. This includes point-to-point availability (the servers were up but the network was down, therefore the service was down).

Most of the biggest cloud vendors use inexpensive hardware for their offerings. They don't put redundancy in each server because they'll just move the instance to another server if that one becomes unavailable. Their redundancy is in servers, not server components. This becomes important if you have a single-server service because they're not going to guarantee that any one server will be highly available. Think of their offerings as "redundant arrays of inexpensive servers". If your service uses a handful of servers or more, their offerings yield high availability (except when they experience cloud issues).

The other point I've implied here but will now state is that you don't care so much about server availability as you do service availability. For single-server services, they're much the same (though you still need to be able to reach that server on the network, too). So, anytime you can provide a service using more than one server (but any one server is capable of providing the service), you're helping mitigate downtime. Even for planned downtime, that can usually be done in rotation, one after the other, so only one of the servers providing the service is down at a time. The service remains available during the server downtimes.

# Appendix 2:
## A Probability Primer

If you've never studied probability and statistics, you may like some help with how to deal with probabilities.

Here's an old example: If you flip a coin, you've got a 50% chance, or 0.5 probability of it coming up heads. If you flip it twice and it comes up heads twice, what's the probability that it'll come up heads again on the third toss? The answer is still 50% or 0.5 probability, because every time you flip it, those are the odds.[10] They do not change based on past history (unless someone is cheating with a two-headed coin, but that's a whole other issue).

Where this comes in for disaster risk is thinking once you've had a disaster, the odds are somehow more against a repeat. Unless you've changed something, the odds of it happening again are exactly the same as when it just happened. The "unless you've changed something" part is important. If you had an electrical fire caused by old wiring that led you to replace all the wiring, not just the area damaged by the fire, you've changed the likelihood of a recurrence.

The lesson here is don't let a recent disaster or lack of one let you become complacent about not having one in the future. In most cases, the odds remain unchanged either way. There are some exceptions. Earthquakes are actually more likely after you've just had one. Afterwards, they like to name them foreshocks or aftershocks around the one largest in magnitude. If you've had flash flooding and get hit by another rain storm, the ground is already saturated and more likely to cause flooding again.

On the other end, another pitfall to avoid is adding up probabilities of unrelated events to come up with a probability that one of them will happen. For example, if you chose twenty events with a 5% chance of occurring, you might add them up and say there's a 100% chance of one of them occurring. This would only be true if they were all probabilities of a single event, say rolling a particular number on a twenty-sided die with each side numbered. There's a 100% chance of rolling a number between 1 and 20, each number with a 5% chance.

If you could actually assign an accurate numeric probability for each disaster type, you could figure out the probability none of them would occur by subtracting each from the number one and then multiplying them together. This gives the odds of not one event and not the other event. So, if you had two events with a 25% chance, the odds that neither will happen are .75 times .75, or 56.25%, making the odds of at least one of them happening 43.75%, not 50% as if you just added them together. The odds for three events with 25% chance yields a 57.81% chance of at least one happening, not 75%.

As a practical matter, you're going to have a hard time assigning accurate numeric values to your disaster probabilities. So, there's not a lot of value in taking your best guesses and applying probability theory to them to attempt to come up with a meaningful number. I'm just trying to show that multiple very low probability events don't necessarily add up to a low probability for one of them to happen, but they can if you have enough of them or they were much closer to "low" than "extremely low".

## About the Author

Harry Flowers has over thirty years of IT experience, almost half of which has been in IT management. As an individual contributor, he has been a software developer, systems engineer, project manager, and infrastructure architect. He has managed all aspects of IT but is usually focused on infrastructure technologies.

Earlier in his career, Harry had been published as an author in technology certification study guides. In 2014, he returned to writing with *Eradicating StupidITy: A Handbook for Smart IT Management.* This book is the second in his management-level series. If you'd like to leave him comments about this book or even another topic you'd like to see treated similarly, feel free to e-mail him at hflowers@leaders4it.com.

# End Notes

First, a short legal statement: **Any trademarks used in this book remain the property of their owners.** Also, **any mention of a company is not an endorsement of their products or services or their fitness for any particular purpose.**

Second, I'd like to give a nod to the U.S. National Institute of Standards and Technology (NIST). The 2002 version of their "NIST Special Publication 800-34", titled "Contingency Planning Guide for Information Technology Systems", helped me get started on this process a decade ago and has greatly influenced how I address disaster recovery planning.

---

[1] This quote has been attributed to both Philip Stanhope, 4th Earl of Chesterfield, and Hunter S. Thompson, author. I think the Earl of Chesterfield wins for saying it first.

[2] Murphy's Law states that anything that can go wrong will go wrong. I'm glad that doesn't actually hold, but it's still good to be prepared for some things to go wrong. The origin of it is a bit murky – there's a nice write-up on Wikipedia if you're interested in the attributions.

[3] Clean agent halocarbon gases were developed to replace Halon as a fire suppressor after it was banned from use because of ozone depletion. You may still have an old Halon system in place; if so, you should probably investigate what it would take to convert it to one of the new gasses in the event the system is triggered. While it's still legal (so far) to refill existing systems, finding Halon to fill it may be difficult and expensive.

[4] Here is a link to the Enhanced Fujita Tornado Intensity Scale: http://www.spc.noaa.gov/faq/tornado/ef-scale.html

[5] From http://oceanservice.noaa.gov/facts/cyclone.html

[6] Here is a link to the Saffir-Simpson Hurricane Wind Scale: http://www.nhc.noaa.gov/aboutsshws.php

[7] In the U.S., the United States Geological Survey is a good source for evaluating earthquake risk information. The following link will let you choose your state: http://www.usgs.gov/science/science.php?term=304

[8] Mobile phones depend on nearby towers for communication. In an area disaster, these will likely suffer the same fate as your business. Satellite phones do not depend on cellular towers, but on satellites orbiting the earth. If you can keep the phone powered, you will still be able to place calls.

[9] I say "should" because, while that's what the standard says, not all DNS implementations are good at honoring this. This could result in the new server not being discovered in DNS lookups longer than planned.

[10] If you want to calculate the odds that three flips will all come up heads before you do any of them, you multiply the probabilities together. So,

0.5*0.5*0.5 gives 0.125, or 12.5% chance of that happening. If you want to calculate the odds that three flips will all match, that is a little trickier. The first flip will come up heads or tails with a probability of 1 (100% chance) – we're not allowing for a chance of the coin standing on its edge or agree to flip again if that's the case. The odds of the second flip coming up to match are 0.5 as is the third flip, making the odds 1*0.5*0.5, or 0.25 probability (25%) chance of all three flips being the same, arbitrarily heads or tails. See, aren't probabilities fun?

www.ingramcontent.com/pod-product-compliance
Lightning Source LLC
Chambersburg PA
CBHW070842180526
45168CB00002B/926